# French Fried: How to Get through Fast Food Alive!!

Brett Coon

# DEDICATION

To the love and support of my family in all things.

# CONTENTS

# ACKNOWLEDGMENTS

To all those who work in the restaurant industry. This is for you.

Hey, how's it going? So, you've decided to check out this guide, huh? That probably means you or someone you know is gearing up for a wild ride in the fast-food biz. Well, guess what? I've been in that game for quite a stretch – seen the highs, the lows, and those "what the heck" moments. I've gone from taking orders to running the show and back again. Now, I've taken it upon myself to drop some knowledge for all you folks stepping into this world for the first time, thinking of making a comeback, or just finding yourself in this crazy maze.

No matter if you're the newbie still figuring things out, the one who's been slingin' burgers for a few weeks, the seasoned pro who's seen it all, or even the one eyeing the exit door, I'm betting my collection of insights into the traps, the office politics circus, and the real-life wisdom I've gathered on this crazy journey will be your secret weapon. So, grab this guide and let's carve out your own path in the "French Fried" adventure. Best of luck out there!

# 1 HUMBLE BEGINNINGS

Alright, listen up. So, you're in a bit of a jam. Maybe your parents are giving you the boot, your bank account's seen better days, bill collectors are ringing you up – that is, until your phone got cut off. Or hey, maybe you just need some extra cash for the holidays or when things slow down at your other gig. Could be you misjudged your retirement fund – who knew, right? Whatever the reason, whether you're a rookie in the job hunt or a seasoned pro, you're on the hunt for that elusive perfect job.

You've been hustling, going from one place to another, hitting up every job site on the internet, and you've probably hit up everyone you know – friends, family, even that guy who lives down the street. Your social media feed's turned into a desperate plea for any lead on a job. But guess what? It's a different ball game now. Unless you've got a buddy in the biz, finding work these days is like a full-time job in itself – and the payoff? Well, disappointment.

Not too long ago, it was simpler. You'd just stroll in all dressed up, drop off your application, give 'em a ring a few days later to nudge for an interview, show up looking like a million bucks, and boom – you'd snag the gig. But welcome to the 21st century, where the job hunt's a straight-up rollercoaster of frustration. You're punching in applications online, interviews are set by managers who might as well be on the moon, and you're waiting for a response like you're waiting for a delayed train.

Then, out of nowhere, your phone buzzes with a number you don't recognize. Heart pounding, you answer, and there it is – a potential lifeline. They want to talk about a position. You're already picturing rubbing it in everyone's faces, telling them you've got a job, you're adulting. But wait a second, who is this again? They repeat themselves, ask if you're still interested, and before you know it, you're blurting out "yes" and locking in an interview. It's like you're in a daze.

And then reality hits you like a ton of bricks. Fast food. Yep, the place you applied to on a whim, the one you were hoping would just ignore you. They're the ones calling you back. It's like the universe has a twisted sense of humor. Out of all your dreams, all the potential jobs, this is what you've got – a gig at a joint in the middle of nowhere.

The name drops like a weight. You're stuck. You can't dodge it anymore. You sigh, tell yourself that "a job's a job," even though you're not buying it. You get real with yourself, start prepping for the inevitable. You set your alarm, dust off that resume, maybe even borrow your old man's Sunday best. You're in for the ride, and it's starting to sink in. Just another day in the life, right? Time to grit your teeth, take a deep breath, and get ready for whatever comes next.

# 2 THE INTERVIEW

Alright, the big day's here. Your nerves are buzzing, though you've kind of steeled yourself for whatever's coming. You walk into the place, no manager in sight, so you just join the line of regular customers waiting at the counter. You've got time to kill, and boy, do you get an eyeful. You see the workers hustling behind the counter, dealing with orders and all sorts of stuff, and the folks in line, they're talking about it too – the chaos behind the scenes, the struggle. It's like getting a sneak peek at your future, a future that's feeling too real already. Finally, after what feels like forever, it's your turn at the counter.

You put on your best "I'm confident-ish" voice and ask, "Hey, is the manager around? I'm here for an interview." The cashier, looking a bit frazzled, lets out a sigh and tells you it's gonna be a minute. Great start. You thank them and stand around, the glares from the other customers and workers making you squirm. Time drags on, and just when you're about to start humming to pass the time, a manager – looking all out of sorts – rushes by. You introduce yourself, ready to shake hands, but they cut you off, asking if you're here for an interview. You fumble a bit but manage a "yes." They tell you to take a seat with the others, hand you a drink cup, and rush off.

"Others?" you mutter to yourself. This isn't shaping up to be a cakewalk. So, you fill your cup and head into the dining area to find the other interviewees. It's like a secret club – the folks with drink cups are your comrades. It takes a bit to spot them amidst the crowd, but you find your place at the table, surrounded by a bunch of people who all look pretty on edge.

Sitting there, you can't help but feel awkward as all eyes seem to be on you. You size up the competition, teens in grubby clothes and adults covered in tattoos. You, on the other hand, are looking sharp – and that gives you a bit of a boost. Confidence creeps back in. But then, another yawn creeps up, time stretching like taffy. Finally, the lunchtime rush dwindles, and the manager makes their appearance. They apologize for the wait, yada yada, and it's time to get this show on the road.

You watch as the others get called in for their interviews, and it's your turn to wait. You're eavesdropping, trying to get a feel for what's coming. The teenagers sound nervous, the middle-aged folks seem to be trying too hard, and then there's that one person who seems more like they belong in a biker gang. You can't help but wonder if they're just buddies with the manager. Doubt starts to gnaw at you, especially considering what kind of job this is.

Finally, it's your moment. The manager arrives, and you go through the motions. They ask questions, you answer – it's like a dance you've practiced a million times. Then they hit you with the "When can you start?" question. You're desperate for work, so you're all in, "ASAP." Next thing you know, you're being told to show up on Saturday for orientation. Saturday, huh? Busy day, but you nod along, trying to look professional.

They're going through the basics – stuff you'll need, what to expect – and you're just nodding away. Then you shake hands, say your goodbyes, and head out. It hits you on the way home: did they just hire everyone? But whatever, you did it! Maybe not the way you expected, but a job's a job... right?

# 3 WELL…YOU GOT IT.

How'd the interview go? Land the job? What's your role? And where's this job again? Brace yourself, because these questions and more are destined to come your way from friends and family, curious about your new gig. But hey, if saying, "Yeah, I snagged a job at Fry King, starting on Saturday for minimum wage," doesn't quite roll off the tongue or align with your pride, don't fret. Allow me to introduce you to some savvy strategies to shine up or add a touch of elegance to your latest adventure. By the end of this chapter, you'll have mastered the art of selecting the right words to transform "just a job" into a thriving and remarkable opportunity!

Let's tackle the most prominent and apparent hurdle first: the name of your workplace. If you're anything like me, announcing that you're working at a fast-food joint isn't exactly your dream reveal. We're all aware of the stereotypes associated with fast food – lazy workers, greasy grub, and paltry paychecks, to name a few. But fear not! There's a glimmer of hope to spare your family the dismay (and your ego the hit). While not all eateries follow this pattern, my worldly exploration has revealed that many of these places are actually franchises, managed and owned by individuals or larger franchise corporations. And that's where your salvation lies. You might be holding down the fort at your local "Burger Bell," but guess what? It could be under the esteemed banner of "Prestige Holdings LLC." So, when the dreaded "where do you work?" question comes knocking, you can confidently respond with, "I'm currently in a front-end position at Prestige Holdings LLC." Not only does this sound impressive, but unless your acquaintances turn into investigative reporters, they're unlikely to dig deeper, leaving them with a rather favorable perception of your achievement.

This leads us right into our second crucial step: job title finesse. Describing your daily duties doesn't have to be a one-way ticket to the grease pit. You'd be amazed by how a touch of creative flair can turn your mundane title into a commanding identifier. A simple "cashier" can metamorphose into a "point-of-sale specialist." Why stick with "line cook" or "grill cook" when you can proudly proclaim your role as a "back-of-house culinary architect"? And even the seemingly routine position of a drive-thru attendant can be elevated to the status of a "QSR (quick-service restaurant) sales expediter." You catch my drift. Unleash your imagination, keep your thesaurus at the ready, and you might even catch your grandparents boasting about their very own culinary architect!

Now, if any of these tactics still have you grappling with that "fast food" aftertaste, here's my top-notch advice: stall, stall, stall! Deflect those questions, take that phantom phone call, make a timely restroom escape – do whatever it takes. But fear not, with your upcoming orientation and first day, you'll have a stockpile of ammo to field the queries from parents and friends. The company is bound to delve into their identity and what sets them apart from the rest, handing you the perfect arsenal to fuel your artful narrative. In no time, your loved ones will be pestering you nonstop to get them a job alongside you, whether you decide to play matchmaker in their job hunt or not – that's on you.

So, there you have it, you've charmed your way into their intrigue, and the entire squad is cheering you on. It's time to hit the sack, rest up for the journey ahead, because tomorrow's your first day and orientation! Sleep well, and may your dreams be sweet.

# 4 SO IT BEGINS...

Cheers! Today marks the dawn of your French Fried journey! But before you dive into the whirlwind of orientation and your very first day, make sure you've got your ducks in a row. Slip-resistant shoes? Check. Clean and pressed work attire? Double-check. Proper identification and requested documents? Well, you know the drill. Pack it all up and head on over – you definitely don't want to be tardy. Oh, and a big welcome to the beginning of your adventure!

As you pull into the parking lot of your fast-food future, you're greeted by a scene that seems straight out of a blockbuster. Every parking spot appears to be claimed, and the drive-thru line is snaking down the street. Your stomach's a mix of nervous excitement and potential panic. Is it the new job jitters or the onset of an impending panic attack? After a deep breath and a quick mental pep talk on why you're here, you psych yourself up for what's to come. You steady yourself, ready to step out of the car and confront the employment storm that awaits.

With determination, you venture forth, navigating through the drive-thru chaos and dodging the vehicular maze. You can practically feel the weight of all eyes on you. A quick glance upward confirms the disapproving stares of the drive-thru queue. Maybe slipping into your work shirt a bit later might have been a better plan, you think to yourself, already sensing the blame for the slow service being heaped on your shoulders before you've even reached the front door.

Finally, you escape the judgmental gaze of the drive-thru and make your way toward the entrance. But just as you're about to reach for the door handle...

"I can't believe they only have two people working..." a woman's exasperated voice erupts as she yanks the door open, sweeping past you along with her family. Their gazes collide with your uniform, and you continue holding the door for them, a silent martyr to the service industry. You're met with a mix of grunts, sighs, eye rolls, and apologetic nods from the family members streaming out. More families follow suit, and as you stand there, you're engulfed in a symphony of chaos – kids screaming, staff shouting order numbers, and the hum of discontented customers.

If war veterans have shell shock, you're pretty sure this is your equivalent – a day that ends in "y." Shaking off the initial sensory overload, you maneuver your way through the chaos, feeling like a salmon swimming upstream. You face mounting resistance from customers who seem to unanimously agree that you're cutting in line – unspoken agreements that you never actually agreed to. Eventually, you make it to the front counter and try to catch the attention of a staff member amidst the frenzy.

"Can I help you?" the breathless, slightly irritated employee manages to grumble out. You mention it's your first day and that you're here for orientation and paperwork. Another eye roll tells you exactly what they think of your intrusion.

"Just a minute," they say, turning to help the next disgruntled customer. You shuffle uncomfortably to the side, desperately avoiding eye contact that might further implicate you as the harbinger of delays. Awkwardly out of place, you start contemplating the universe's mysteries while waiting for your turn.

But then, amidst the chaos, you spot an employee in a button-up shirt dashing behind the counter. A swift exchange with the cashier ends with a gesture in your direction. The "manager?" shakes his head, enters and exits a small office, then makes his way toward you with a soda cup and a stack of papers.

"Hey, sorry about the chaos. We're slammed right now. Grab a drink and start filling out these papers with the other folks here for orientation," he says with a casual wave toward the sea of customers. You glance over and see a small group of lost souls clutching drinks. As quickly as he arrives, he's off to the next task.

With a resigned sigh, you fill your cup and navigate the crowd, making brief nods to fellow newcomers along the way. You settle at a back table, surrounded by your comrades-in-orientation, and delve into the paperwork.

"Sorry about the wait, folks. How about we wrap up this paperwork and then I'll take you on a whirlwind tour of the joint?" Your manager's back, and with a quick shuffle, you join the line and embark on the grand tour. You get quick rundowns of various spots – break room, schedule, kitchen, freezer, and the like. Some staff members offer curt nods or casual grunts, their interactions shaped by the intensity of the day's business.

After the tour, you find a little-used corner to hunker down and complete the tedious paperwork and tax spiel. It's a mind-numbing process filled with questions that the manager can't answer thanks to "legal reasons." You cross your fingers, submit the paperwork, and offer up a silent prayer for a smooth process.

And there you have it – your first steps into employment, marked by paperwork and a whirlwind tour. Depending on how the establishment's managed, you could be in for some coaching, computer learning modules, and a guided hands-on training experience that helps you grasp the store's processes and expectations. Alternatively, you might receive a quick and casual overview of policies and procedures, a smidge of hands-on guidance from kind-hearted staff, and then the baptism by fire as you navigate your way through a shift – irritating both colleagues and customers alike. It's a rollercoaster, and you're holding on tight.

No matter what path unfolds before you, your orientation has set the tone for your days ahead. Stressful or smooth, easy or exasperating, the payroll beckons, and that's your calling card. So, return home, prep that alarm clock, get your uniform ready, and indulge in whatever rituals help dull the edges of reality. Tomorrow's a fresh day, and as the rumor mill goes – from friends, family, coworkers, and those self-help sites – things will smooth out, and you'll find your groove. Or so they say, right?

# 5 FIRST DAY OF FOREVER

Emerging from the shattered fragments of your dreamscape, you're jolted awake by the relentless clangs and squeals of an alarm that you've already snoozed five times. With a burst of adrenaline, you catapult out of bed and swiftly get yourself in order, mentally gearing up for the day ahead. This is your moment, the grand unveiling. Time to put that orientation knowledge to the test, present your uniform in all its clean, wrinkle-free glory, and dazzle them with your punctuality, arriving a whole fifteen minutes early for your shift. You've got this. Just take a deep breath, hold your head high, and stride through those doors...

"Hey, it's my first day..." you utter with a mix of exclamation and uncertainty, directing your words at a disinterested staff member who was conspicuously absent during your previous shift. They mutter something barely intelligible while fixating on the same spot they've been wiping repeatedly. After a few awkward beats, their glazed expression gradually transforms back into a semblance of the hardworking individual they might have been in some distant past.

"Let me get the manager."

Another staff member, sporting a similar button-up shirt or a slightly different colored polo, comes over. "What's your name?" they inquire. As you share your information, you catch them muttering under their breath, "I wish I would have known I was training someone today." They nod an acknowledgment, inquire about your clock-in number if it was established yesterday (or lack thereof if they were caught off guard and promised to fix your time later), and then you're either clocking in or jotting down your time. Et voilà, off you go on another store tour – a replay of the identical store tour from the day before. It's déjà vu all over again, as you traverse the same paths, reacquaint yourself with the same locales, and hear the same spiel about various job positions. You can practically see the pattern forming, but hold on, don't jump the gun just yet.

I know what you're thinking – your instincts are buzzing, urging you to speak up and reveal that this information has already been covered. But, oh dear shlub, for the sake of your financial safety and the longevity of your fledgling career, I implore you to suppress this epiphany. Because, after weathering years of these fast food escapades, you'll realize that the overlords of these quick-service domains are propelled primarily by their egos. They've staked their claim on these street corners, cocooned in the illusion of constant knowledge, unerring correctness, and being the supreme authorities. If you dare disturb the delicate equilibrium of their egotistical thrones, challenge their assumed omnipotence in even the slightest way, you're setting off a chain reaction that spells your own downfall. They'll label you as a pet of another manager, a threat to their dominion, and worse, you'll have spotlighted their potential inability to grasp the store's day-to-day nuances. They're already visibly (and audibly) irritated, so for the sake of your financial stability, follow the script from the previous shift. You nod and acquiesce, obediently embracing the tasks of the day. You're led along, attempting each task as it's presented, desperately avoiding becoming the bottleneck in the production line, and fervently wishing for the clock to tick just a bit faster.

Gradually, you muster the courage to ask questions. Your inquiries become bolder as you slowly grasp the mechanics of the fast food universe. Your efforts start to get under your trainer's skin, but you find a kernel of pride in your small triumphs. They even begin receiving compliments on their ability to show you the ropes, and you relish in these meager victories. Then, before you know it... you're left at the front counter all by your lonesome.

Oh no, panic whispers in your mind. You scan the surroundings, peering around corners, seeking refuge in the kitchen, and scouting out the backroom. You spot it – the van pulling up. Your heart races, and you hasten your search, urgently calling out for someone – anyone – as you peer around the kitchen and office. And there it is, ajar – the forbidden door. Throughout all previous tours, they've drilled into you that this door remains closed for safety, save for trash disposal or accepting deliveries in the company of a manager. But there it is, a crack of light tempting you, while the customer uproar rises like a storm. You're running out of options. You throw caution to the wind and crack that door open, taking on whatever consequences might lie beyond.

And just like that, the mystery unfolds. You peek around the corner and there they are – the entire staff, smoking cigarettes, glued to their phones, a congregation of rule-breakers seemingly oblivious to the mounting tide of irate customers in the lobby. They lock eyes with you, a guilty bunch caught red-handed in their covert gathering. Their stares question your intentions, as if you've stumbled upon some secret gathering. An awkward silence is broken by your anxious explanation. The collective sigh, mixed with grumbling and eye rolls, orders you to get back inside – back to the brewing tempest that awaits. You gulp and resign yourself to your fate.

As they swoop in to take charge, you retreat to the background, wishing you could meld into the scenery. The rush finally subsides, and you muster the courage to ask your manager for a break – a respite from the ordeal. But your request is met with a smug reply, denying breaks due to busyness and legal loopholes. The shock lingers as they strut away, leaving you stunned. You wander back to your station, a wounded spirit seething with the injustice of it all. It stings. You put in the same hours, worked just as hard with the limited knowledge you had, while they were outside, shirking rules. The bitter taste of unfairness weighs heavy on your mind.

As you clean up and clock out, your thoughts are consumed by the day's events, their smug remarks, and a vow to right these wrongs — somehow.

# 6 THE ART OF THE BREAK

*No Time for Rest? No Problem!*

The restaurant industry has a notorious reputation for being stingy with shift breaks and reluctant to grant requested time off, regardless of the notice given. The reasons behind this practice are often rooted in legal considerations, staffing challenges, and a management culture that can hinder the enforcement of break policies. However, fear not, for within this chapter lies a treasure trove of strategies to carve out those much-needed moments of respite from the grind of the culinary world. While the road may seem closed, I assure you that there are ways to navigate around this seemingly impenetrable barrier. Presented here are some proven methods to navigate your way through the maze of restaurant work, offering you a chance to catch your breath amidst the chaos.

# Smoke Up, Johnny:

*Joining the Fumes for Freedom*

Starting off, let's revisit a technique that has stood the test of time and experience. If you're seeking an almost foolproof escape from the monotony of your workday, consider lighting up a cigarette – metaphorically speaking, of course. Despite a company's rules, principles, or policies, the ubiquitous smoke break tends to infiltrate every level of the restaurant hierarchy. From fresh-faced new hires to the loftiest echelons of management, the allure of the smoke break is undeniable.

In the confined universe of a restaurant, you'll witness the covert dash of staff to the back door, the flicker of a coat behind a dumpster, the muffled cough from around the corner, and the telltale scent of smoke trailing crew members as they reenter. If you want in on this clandestine fraternity, simply seize the moment. When your coworkers step out for a smoke, take the initiative to join them. A simple request like, "Hey, mind if I join you?" is often met with empathetic nods and sighs, as fellow comrades understand the trials and tribulations of the culinary life. Soon, you'll find yourself acquiring your own pack of cigarettes and partaking in these periodic escapes like a seasoned veteran.

However, let's not be blinded by the allure of this path. While it may be the easiest way to ensure breaks, it's hardly the wisest decision for your health and career. Frequent smoke breaks can negatively impact your work quality and efficiency, and the addictive nature of smoking can exacerbate the emotional stress of a customer service role. Worse yet, smoking can be wielded as a tool of control and degradation, often by those in authority nursing grudges or harboring resentment. Certain employees (or friends, or those in management's good graces) might enjoy more extended and frequent smoke breaks, leaving their colleagues to shoulder the extra workload and stress, unfairly dividing the burden.

What's more, if a complaint arises, the company's long-forgotten policies may suddenly be enforced with newfound vigor, yet seldom will the worst offenders – sometimes even management – bear the brunt of these reprimands. Should you dare confront management or challenge their status quo, they might engineer your unjust dismissal, cloaked in a smokescreen of "no smoking" policy adherence. For those embarking on this route, my advice is to play by the manager's rules, stay discreet, and perhaps even document a few infractions to safeguard your own position.

# Fake It till You Make It:

## *Theatrics for Time Off*

Another method, albeit far more devious, involves feigning illness or ailment. I've both employed and witnessed this technique, with varying degrees of success. To execute this scheme, you must fully commit to the act, portraying anything from low blood sugar necessitating a snack, to medication that requires a brief interval of rest, to recurring medical appointments with conveniently similar notes.

The efficacy of this method hinges on your commitment to the ruse. Whether you're new on the job or mid-season "contracting" the ailment, the depth of your acting skills will determine your triumph. Initially, expect skepticism and possibly a request for a doctor's note, especially if your manager is prone to mistrust. In this case, having a physician's note, or even an altered one, in your back pocket might be prudent.

Here's the twist – managers are often preoccupied with sales figures, labor costs, and avoiding direct customer interactions. Avoid raising red flags, and they'll usually accept your information at face value. For instance, they might not investigate your doctor's note further, choosing to avoid extra work that could deflate their ego or expose their lack of investigative skills.

A word of caution: any slip-ups or braggadocio could lead to increased scrutiny. This method is not for the faint of heart or the risk-averse. If your job hangs in the balance, this approach courts failure daily if you're faced with too many questions.

# Blackmail:

## *Playing the Favoritism Game*

The final strategy I'll share is a daring one, with limited chances of success. However, if you manage to pull it off, you'll unlock the doors to a workplace paradise. Simply put, you aim to cultivate a relationship or foster a sense of favoritism with your superiors. This method is slightly more challenging for men than women, although some women managers might engage in unprofessional relationships just as some men do. If you're fortunate enough to capture your manager's attention successfully, this approach will bestow upon you an entirely different work experience.

Your rewards will range from easier tasks, more breaks, complimentary items, and possibly even a raise. However, alongside these benefits, you'll earn the distrustful respect of your colleagues. The most intriguing part? Once you've breached your manager's defenses and embarked on this unprofessional path, you can exert control. Threatening to go to Human Resources if you don't get your way can grant you a level of impunity that others lack, essentially coasting through your employment under the gossamer wings of blackmail.

Yet, navigating matters of the heart is a treacherous path. Like any relationship, you might develop feelings deeper than expected — feelings stronger than those of your target. If you fail to reverse the situation, you could find yourself pining for your boss, who has lost interest, thereby nullifying your blackmail potential. Tread lightly, for this method, though high-risk, presents the promise of high reward.

# 7 Navigating the Culinary Maze: Unveiling the Dynamics of Your "Family"

*Venturing Deeper into the Heart of Your Culinary Odyssey*

As you continue along your French Fried journey, you've likely spent numerous shifts within the confines of your newfound haven — a place that may have become more endurable with well-timed breaks, if you've played your cards right. Throughout your days in this culinary labyrinth, you've undoubtedly had ample opportunities to cross paths with your fellow employees, each bringing their unique approach and attitude to the collective endeavor. While you may have observed these differences, what you've witnessed merely scratches the surface of the intricate web that is this minimum-wage existence. Beneath the surface lies a sinister tapestry of ulterior motives and manipulations, a realm that could ensnare you in its grip if you let your guard down. So, you've likely heard the term "family" or "team" to describe your workplace, either from a manager or a handbook during your initial training days. In order to prevent you from descending into the abyss of anguish and turmoil, I'm here to offer you insights into the "family" you'll encounter during your employment – their true intentions, and how to skillfully navigate the fine line between camaraderie and catastrophe.

# Enter the Hen!

## *Wisdom and Warnings of the Nest's Matriarch*

Early in your tenure, you'll likely cross paths with the Hen. This seasoned worker, often more mature than the typical crew, occupies a role in the daytime kitchen or front counter. While their knowledge is valuable, their demeanor can be testy, and their willingness to share insights may be limited. If you manage to earn the Hen's favor, you'll gain a significant advantage – their approval can translate into favorable treatment from both staff and management. But be cautious; should you unintentionally slight the Hen, their accumulated years of experience could come crashing down upon you with overwhelming force.

Why the moniker "Hen"? Think of the chicken or "hen" – a creature that goes about its business with a certain tranquility, unless something goes awry. In that instant, it transforms into a squawking force of nature, persistently demanding order be restored. This same temperament often emerges in the workplace. Befriend the Hen, and you'll find yourself welcomed into their circle, leading to smoother workdays despite occasional annoyances.

But tread carefully, for any slight, no matter how minor, can trigger a cascade of complaints both among the general staff and to management. The Hen, who has had numerous opportunities to bond with coworkers, will not hesitate to make their grievances known. Managers, aware that ignoring their concerns could lead to relentless squawking, will take action to soothe the Hen's agitation. To engage with the Hen effectively, maintain a low profile, nod and smile, and avoid situations that could ruffle their feathers. If you inadvertently become a source of their displeasure, brace yourself for their vociferous disapproval, both within the staff and with management.

# The Lovers

## *Entwined Objectives: Uniting the Motivated Pair*

When considering the term "lovers," it's essential to broaden your understanding beyond romantic entanglements. In our context, it refers to any two employees, regardless of their relationship status, who collaborate to advance mutual goals, whether in plain sight or behind the scenes. You've probably encountered company policies discouraging or even prohibiting such associations due to valid concerns. While couples or friends can be effective teams that contribute to excellence, when their personal ambitions take precedence, it can prove detrimental to the business.

The driving force behind the "lovers" is their self-interest. They may collaborate to the point of wasting hours on the clock with camaraderie, clocking each other in or covering shifts without informing management, thus costing the company undue expenses. If their objectives are less than noble, they might conspire to spread dissent among the staff or even undermine management.

The hierarchy within a "lover" partnership can exacerbate the situation, especially when one wields authority over the other. You may have noticed employees who seem impervious to reprimands despite tardiness or poor job performance – this could be due to their ties with other staff. Remember, the "lovers" will consistently prioritize their interests, rendering you a subordinate figure by comparison.

While I've witnessed instances where family or friends successfully manage a restaurant, there's another side to the coin. My advice regarding the "lovers"? Keep your distance unless you're ready to be swept into a maelstrom of drama. Their partnership may yield short-term benefits, but more often than not, they'll turn against other staff or manipulate coworkers to their advantage, causing you to suffer the collateral damage.

# She's A Killer, Queen!

*Navigating the Drama Queen's Web*

Allow me to introduce the Drama Queen – an employee who warrants special attention. This archetype holds attributes that might resonate with various coworkers, but it's paramount to delve into their traits, both positive and negative, to understand the perils of close association.

Identifying a Drama Queen isn't as tricky as it may seem. You can craft a hypothetical story and share it within earshot of your target. If they immediately spring into a tale of their own woes, you've likely found a Drama Queen. Study their interactions – observe how they react to preferential treatment or unfair situations, and you'll note their tendency to exaggerate and overreact. They will spin situations out of proportion, sowing discord and division among the staff, often under the pretense of defending their own interests.

But why the drama? Drama Queens often involve themselves in others' lives to fill personal voids, and the consequences — whether coworkers' anger, frustration, or even job loss — are secondary to the thrill they derive from inciting reactions. These individuals prioritize themselves above all else, and their actions, no matter how disruptive, satisfy their need for significance.

However, Drama Queens are bound to unravel their web of deception. Eventually, they alienate those around them, exposing their manipulative tactics. Exile, whether self-imposed or through termination, is inevitable. When the dust settles, the wreckage becomes evident, leaving those entangled in their schemes to regret their involvement.

# The Dreaded Grublak!

*Confronting the Master Manipulator*

Finally, meet the Grublak – a creature dreaded in the restaurant realm. This manipulative force emerges sporadically, wreaking havoc upon both employees and managers alike. Usually female, the Grublak emerges from the darkest depths, worming their way into the confidence of the management team, leveraging manipulation and deceit.

One unmistakable trait is their tendency to overshare personal information without prompting, especially in the initial interactions. As you spend more time with them, you'll notice inconsistencies in their stories, revealing their propensity for deceit. Their nefarious intentions unfold when they fabricate rules and procedures to exert control. The danger intensifies if they secure the loyalty of upper management by feigning respect and loyalty.

Once in control, the Grublak manipulates situations to strengthen their position, replacing dissenting staff with those more pliable. The result? A warped reality where their deceit reigns supreme, while experienced staff are systematically replaced to maintain their control. Only a united front of brave individuals can dismantle this web of deception, preserving the integrity of the workplace.

# Navigating the Labyrinth

As you navigate the culinary labyrinth, armed with insights into the characters you'll encounter, remember that survival hinges on discretion and wisdom. Engage cautiously with the Hen, maintain a safe distance from the "lovers," avoid the Drama Queen's snares, and stand strong against the Grublak's manipulation. By mastering these strategies, you can elevate your experience, safeguarding yourself from the pitfalls that may lie ahead.

# 8 The Boss Man Cometh:

# Navigating the Management Jungle

*Insights into the Enigmatic Leaders of Your Culinary Empire*

As you continue your culinary voyage, it's essential to understand not only your fellow staff members but also the leaders who wield power over your daily existence. This chapter unveils the diverse array of management personas that may cross your path, providing insights into their intentions and strategies. So, let's dive into the world of restaurant management and explore the characters you're likely to encounter in your workplace "family."

# The Comedian: A Laughing Matter

*When Chuckles Become Chains*

Meet the Comedian, a management style that thrives on a laid-back, friendly approach. Working with this character might seem like a never-ending party, with bending of rules and relaxed attitudes creating a fun work environment. The Comedian believes in the adage "a happy staff is a successful staff," often leading to enjoyable shifts filled with camaraderie.

However, the Comedian's downfall lies in their leniency, which can backfire when company policies tighten. As they transition from the cool boss to the "Boss" boss, they struggle to enforce rules they previously ignored. This sudden shift in enforcement creates confusion, leading to increased inefficiency and theft. Their reign of merriment devolves into a strict, authoritarian stance, leaving staff disoriented and disappointed. This shift from friend to foe results in an unfortunate lose-lose scenario, ultimately damaging their standing and the bonds they once cherished.

# The Warlord: Ruler by Fear

*Conquering Through Intimidation*

Enter the Warlord, a manager who wields authority through fear. This tyrant relies on intimidation, instilling a constant sense of impending failure or termination in their staff. Their modus operandi is rooted in recognizing the staff's dependence on their jobs, using this vulnerability to control and manipulate.

While the Warlord's approach may yield short-term compliance, their reign faces a pivotal weakness – an uprising of staff. One employee's dissent can trigger a mass exodus, leading to an influx of stress on the remaining team members and more mistakes. This snowball effect weakens the Warlord's control, potentially resulting in their resignation, demotion, or firing. Their tactics prove unsustainable in the face of a united and resilient staff.

# The Sneaky Snake: Master of Deceit

## *Whispers and Manipulation*

Now, meet the Sneaky Snake, a master of manipulation and deceit. This manager portrays themselves as a confidante, eliciting staff's personal stories and secrets under the guise of friendship. Yet, their true intent is to gather ammunition to undermine and belittle employees, fostering an atmosphere of mistrust and discord.

The Snake's power lies in their ability to exploit the divisions they've sown. By using staff secrets against them, they maintain control while pitting employees against each other. However, this web of intrigue inevitably unravels. A single act of rebellion can expose their tactics, leading to their eventual downfall as staff bands together against the manipulation.

# Long Live the King!!!

## *The Monarch of Ego*

Last but not least, let's explore the King, a manager who exudes self-indulgent authority. This figure revels in the benefits of their position, delegating tasks and responsibilities to their subordinates. They strategically involve themselves only in high-impact situations, maintaining an image of control and confidence.

The King's vulnerability arises from their reluctance to address minor issues. Their reactive approach often leads to escalating problems that could have been prevented. When these problems culminate, they resort to blame-shifting, seeking scapegoats to resolve the consequences of their inaction. This complacent leadership style, though seemingly enduring, ultimately leads to their dethroning as their laissez-faire attitude undermines their success.

# Surviving the Management Jungle

As you navigate the management landscape, remember that each persona comes with strengths and weaknesses. The Comedian's joviality may turn to rigid enforcement, the Warlord's fear-based control can crumble with a united staff, the Sneaky Snake's manipulations can be dismantled by courageous individuals, and the King's indulgence may lead to their downfall. Approach each management style with caution, adaptability, and the knowledge that, ultimately, their reigns are not impervious to change.

# 9 FRENCH FRIED HOMICIDE:

*Unraveling the Unsanitary Truths Behind the Counter*

As you delve further into the fast food world, it's crucial to open your eyes to the unsavory realities that often lurk behind the scenes. Despite the priority placed on return business, health codes, and hygiene policies, the underbelly of the industry often reveals a stark contrast. Brace yourself as we navigate through some of the most unsettling violations and practices you might encounter in the fast food realm.

# Preparation "F": A Recipe for Disaster

## *Frozen to Fire Danger*

One would expect that proper food preparation and storage practices are paramount in a food-based industry. However, the pressure of high-volume rushes and inadequate prep often leads to shortcuts that violate food safety standards. Quick-thawing frozen items on counters, in hot water pans, or under heat lamps violates the temperature danger zone and exposes food to harmful bacteria growth. Items like raw chicken, dairy, and beef are often left unattended for hours during busy shifts or put back in the fridge, only to be used without proper cooldown. Even food deliveries are left sitting on the floor for extended periods. Although health regulations exist to prevent such practices, speed often triumphs over safety.

While addressing these concerns might seem like a noble endeavor, voicing them to management could be met with indifference, hostility, or even retaliation from your co-workers. Many employees might believe that speaking up won't make a difference due to the pervasive neglect of proper food safety techniques. Nevertheless, focusing on your own actions and adhering to safe practices is a step toward protecting customers from potential illness.

# The Necessities of Proper Hygiene:

## *Cleanliness as a Mirage*

Proper hygiene and personal appearance are often emphasized in employee handbooks, but reality can be strikingly different. Many staff members, including managers, sometimes show up with unkempt appearances, emanating odors of sweat and last night's festivities. The requirement to wash hands, while well-documented, is frequently reduced to a mere rinse or cursory wipe, casting aside health guidelines in favor of speed and convenience. This negligence in proper handwashing becomes evident in the fast-paced environment, where customer demands take precedence over hygiene protocols.

Addressing these discrepancies might be a futile endeavor, as many managers fail to practice what they preach. Expecting a change in this culture could result in disappointment, making it crucial to remain committed to your personal hygiene and following proper procedures, regardless of others' actions.

# Sickness, Shmickness

*Get to Work Faker!!!*

One of the most disturbing practices within the fast food industry is the manipulation of staff to work even when they're unwell. High turnover rates and the reliance on these jobs for financial survival create a power dynamic where employees are coerced into coming to work, even if they are sick. The management's primary concern is maintaining operational efficiency, often disregarding the health risks to both employees and customers. Many employees find themselves working with contagious illnesses, vomiting, fever, or diarrhea, all of which pose a significant threat to food safety and public health.

While company policies may dictate that employees must find replacements or provide doctor's notes, these requirements are often unrealistic, especially for those struggling financially. Employees are caught in a dilemma where their livelihoods are at stake, leading to the spread of illness among staff and customers. In many cases, voicing concerns to management might lead to write-ups, penalties, or even termination.

# Facing the Fast Food Reality

The fast food industry's grim realities expose a glaring disconnect between stated values and actual practices. The pressures of high demand, staff turnover, and financial constraints often lead to the neglect of food safety and employee well-being. Voicing concerns might result in indifference or retaliation, making it essential to focus on your actions and uphold personal standards of hygiene and safety. As you navigate this environment, remember that change begins with individuals who are committed to upholding principles, even when the system seems resistant to reform.

# 10 SERVICE WITH A SMILE!!! (OR SUFFER THE CONSEQUENCES)

*Navigating the Colorful Characters of the Customer Realm*

While the fast food world might appear rife with challenges and

disheartening realities, don't despair just yet. Amidst the chaos, there

lies a glimmer of positivity and even amusement. As you embark on this culinary journey, remember that there's more to it than just a paycheck – there are unique characters, both customers and coworkers, who can make the experience surprisingly memorable. So, let's delve into some customer archetypes you might encounter and those you wish had existed during your own trials and tribulations.

# The Snoot:

## *Complaining for Complaining's Sake*

Meet the Snoot, the customer who turns even a glowing experience into a source of criticism. They may initially shower praise on the staff, food, and service, only to pull the manager aside later and express their dissatisfaction with the absence of smiles from the team. These elusive creatures thrive on nitpicking, finding fault in even the most impeccable transactions. Dealing with Snoots can be perplexing, as they don't seek material compensation – their complaints are their currency. This breed of customer often leaves damaging feedback, which management takes as gospel. How does one respond to such a conundrum? The truth is, even managers struggle with this breed of customer, making them one of the most mystifying entities in the customer service landscape.

# The Misguided Majesty, Mistress Karen: A Force to be Reckoned With

## *The Royal Treatment*

Enter the Misguided Majesty, also known as Karen, a customer fueled by entitlement. Rational explanations are futile when they demand to speak to the manager, their manager, and their manager's manager over the slightest inconveniences. Their high expectations are immune to understaffing, stock shortages, or regional menu differences. The phrases "clean these filthy tables," "let me talk to your manager," and "this is unacceptable" are their anthem. To serve them effectively, one must bow to their demands, ensuring their $5 combo is delivered on a virtual golden platter. Crossing their path unscathed requires mastering the art of exceptional service but be warned – the task is herculean.

# The Picky Eater: Chasing the Impossible Standard

## *Perfection in Every Bite*

Behold the Picky Eater, an enigma who entrusts their culinary destiny to others while holding unattainable standards. They'll take "no pickle" to a whole new realm, critiquing the fries' crispiness, burger tenderness, and even the accuracy of their telepathic requests. It's a delicate dance of trying to meet their French Fried perfection before they believe a refund is warranted. Escaping their wrath requires lightning-fast reflexes in passing them off to managers or other staff members who can expertly navigate their unique dietary demands.

# The "Irregular" Regular: Friend and Foe

## *A Tale of Two Regulars*

Regulars, the lifeblood of any restaurant, can be a double-edged sword. On one hand, they can infuse joy into the most mundane days, with their pleasant demeanors and understanding of the occasional mistake. On the other hand, the "irregular" regulars create an unending cycle of dissatisfaction. Ordering the same thing each time, they expect a different outcome, leading to recurring complaints. These enigmatic figures seem to thrive on misery, revisiting the same issues yet expecting different results. This dichotomy can be both a blessing and a curse in the fast food universe.

# The Scamburglar: Master of Deception

*A Game of Lies and Gains*

Lastly, the Scamburglar represents a cunning customer who aims to manipulate staff and management for their gain. With an arsenal of lies and deception, they concoct stories to extract freebies, going to extreme lengths to create a façade of mistreatment. From exaggerations to false accusations, they weave a web of deceit. As staff members question the validity of their claims, the intricacies of their stories begin to unravel. These connoisseurs of manipulation escalate their tactics until they achieve their desired outcome. Dealing with a

Scamburglar is akin to a battle of wits, where recognizing their tactics is the first step in thwarting their schemes.

## Embrace the Circus of Characters

As you navigate the fast food world, remember that it's not just about food and efficiency – it's a colorful tapestry of characters and experiences. While you may encounter the Snoots, Karens, Picky Eaters, "Irregular" Regulars, and Scamburglars, keep in mind that these personas contribute to the rich tapestry of your journey. Embrace the chaos, learn from it, and carry the lessons into your future endeavors. After all, the characters you meet today might just be the anecdotes you share tomorrow.

# 11 THE FINAL COUNTDOWN

*Reaching the Breaking Point*

Have you endured your fair share of difficult customers? Felt the weight of unjust treatment from management? Is your spirit worn down, your energy depleted, and your heart heavy? Welcome to the inevitable conclusion of your fast food journey – the breaking point. Whether you've endured a few weeks or years, this breaking point will find you. It could be triggered by one last obnoxious customer, a manager's final unreasonable demand, or a new policy that tips you over the edge.

So, now that you've reached this crossroads, how do you navigate your exit? Will you go out with a bang, leaving a mess in your wake? Perhaps you'll confront a manager or customer with your pent-up frustrations, sabotage a shift, or simply fade into oblivion by not showing up. The choice is yours.

## Here's my two cents:

If revenge won't bring you true satisfaction, if retaliation will only add to your own misery, then take the high road. These companies will replace you in no time, and seeking retribution won't grant you the peace you're seeking. They view their employees as expendable pawns in the grand game of profit. Your time is better spent moving on to better things.

# Hold… Almost… Drum Roll, Please!

As we inch closer to the culmination of your fast food journey, let's take a moment to appreciate the little perks that might have sweetened the deal – employee discounts or free meals, perhaps? And paid time off – though rare – could provide some respite. But let's be honest, those are mere crumbs in the grand feast of life.

# And…Congratulations!!!

If you've traversed this guide to its conclusion, you've successfully navigated the treacherous landscape of fast food employment. You've glimpsed the truth behind this modern form of servitude, witnessed the darkest aspects of human behavior, and emerged with lessons that even your worst enemy wouldn't envy.

Where do you go from here? The path is yours to forge. Even if you're reading this from behind bars, you can still glean insights from this guide to shape a brighter tomorrow. It's time to acknowledge that life offers more than a paycheck and enduring the mistreatment of those who thrive in these abysses. The time you've lost to this role – time away from the joys and marvels the world has to offer – is irreplaceable.

The anger, stress, and anxiety you've borne daily chip away at your confidence and hope until you question your own potential. Living in an environment where replaceability is the norm and gratitude is fleeting can corrode your spirit and shatter your psyche. As you close this chapter, remember that the lessons you've learned are yours to keep, and the time has come for my parting words...

# Do Not Settle for Less

Reject the jobs that demand you choose between your family, health, and job security.

Reject the idea that you must sacrifice your presence during times of need. These jobs manipulate you into believing you're honor-bound to serve those who care more about uninterrupted shifts than your well-being. The companies don't care about you, just the dollars you bring.

I implore you – break free from the ranks, abandon a life of mediocrity traded for bills paid.

 Pursue your dreams, even if some scoff at your choice. Money isn't everything; there's a world beyond. Don't poison yourself with monotonous expectations. Don't wage futile battles in small worlds surrounded by parking lots. Seize the life that awaits you.

Success isn't guaranteed in this pursuit, nor is a life devoid of hardships. But you can seek a career and existence that allows you to savor family moments without fear, where pursuing your dreams isn't considered a betrayal. Today, take that first step, and wherever it leads, hold onto it, and move forward – do not look back.

# Here's to Life, Love, and Pursuing Happiness!

**Remember, you can find stability and keep your dreams alive, even through adversity. You're breaking free from the chains that have held you back.**

**Congrats, my friend, for surviving the journey of a life that's been "French Fried"!**

This Book is dedicated to the living hell that exists within the **QSR** (fast food) industry.

To the money-grubbing tyrannical scraps of humanity who run these companies under the guise of family, religion, or righteousness.

To the customers who carry themselves with the privilege of kings over a few dollars of processed garbage.

To the poor souls who are trapped in these positions either by fate, disability, or poor life choices.

And to the destruction of these enclosed kingdoms: where men and women think themselves gods, manipulating lives based on invented and imagined slights to their rule, and who are nothing outside of the building in which they make their domain.


French Fried:

How to Get Through Fast Food Alive!!!

# ABOUT THE AUTHOR

Born in Iowa at the start of the '90s, this author fell in love with literature from an early age. Since opening that first book, the magic of storytelling and the written word has captured his heart. Now, with his own little rascal and a loving partner, he aspires to pass on his passion for reading and writing to his child.

As a dedicated author and parent, he draws inspiration from the boundless love of his family. This support fuels his creativity, motivating him to craft stories that resonate with readers of all ages.

Throughout his literary journey, he has honed his craft, developing a writing style that stimulates minds and evokes genuine emotions. His prose weaves together intricate narratives, sharing the joy of the written word cherished over the years.

With a twinkle in his eye and an ink-stained pen in hand, he endeavors to bring readers to tears, impart joy, enlighten souls, and engage minds. His ultimate goal is to create stories that leave a lasting impact, stirring the imagination and touching the very core of the human experience.

A versatile writer, he delves into multiple genres, from heartwarming romances to thrilling adventures and captivating mysteries. He finds joy in exploring diverse worlds and characters, each offering a unique perspective on life.

When not immersed in fiction, he cherishes quality moments with his family, explores the great outdoors, or embarks on new literary adventures that fuel his creativity.

Through his writing, he invites readers on unforgettable journeys, promising tales that leave indelible marks on hearts and minds. He eagerly looks forward to sharing his literary escapades with the world, one heartfelt story at a time.

www.ingramcontent.com/pod-product-compliance
Lightning Source LLC
Chambersburg PA
CBHW071054260726
48661CB00006B/2266